50 Exciting ideas for using
Super Heroes and Popular Culture

ACKNOWLEDGEMENTS

Written by: Anni McTavish

Illustrated by: Peter Scott

Produced by: Lynda Lawrence

Published by: Lawrence Educational
Unit 21, Brookvale Trading Estate,
Birmingham B6 7AQ

© Lawrence Educational 2009

ISBN: 978-1-903670-79-8

CONTENTS

Introduction

The ideas in this book are a starting point for exploring and responding to children's interest in super heroes and popular culture. Many of the ideas will support you in dealing creatively with behaviour, and engage more deeply with children's fascination with these themes.

The ideas can be developed both indoors and out. Over the years, I have enjoyed many interesting and thought provoking conversations with practitioners in workshops I've run. Some of the ideas discussed and generously shared are included in this book.

Involving parents and building relationships with them will be supported by acknowledging their children's passions, sharing our expertise about learning, and inviting them to contribute by donating junk modelling materials etc. Other resources can be found cheaply in £1 stores or in supermarkets, and materials can be gathered from household objects, scrap projects or wholesale stationers. Primary and Secondary School jumble sales are often a rich hunting ground for small world resources, dressing-up and popular culture figures, as well as comics and second hand books.

Children have a real need to explore and act out their experiences and feelings, and they will engage in superhero and popular culture play for a number of different reasons – to explore identity, gender, and issues around power and control, or simply to try out a different role. They may also be curious about death, and want to explore it in a way that isn't too scary. Superhero play can also be about testing physicality and developing skills for conflict resolution, negotiation and problem solving.

Sometimes, the scenarios that children create will include gun and weapon play, and we may feel challenged as practitioners to find appropriate and responsible ways to respond. Gun and weapon play is a much debated issue, and with this in mind there is a further reading list towards the back of the book. In particular, Penny Holland's book, 'We don't play with guns here' (2003), based on her research of weapon play in early years settings and Tina Hyder's book 'War, Conflict and Play' (2005), both in the Debating Play Series edited by Tina Bruce, are excellent background reading. It can be a useful exercise as a staff group to discuss these issues, and develop a policy to support good practice. To help with this, you will find a sample Superhero/weapon play policy at the back of the book.

Children will need time to explore the materials and ideas. They might use them in a different way from the one you intended, therefore you may need to change some, and also rethink the 'further possibilities' ideas. In some cases, it may be appropriate to support the children by becoming a partner in the play. Taking time to do this will help you to see more of 'what's under the surface' - what concepts and questions children are really exploring. Above all, enjoyment and fun will be part of this play and creativity together.

Anni McTavish

Idea 1

Superhero Sets

What you need:
Comics, wrapping paper with superhero/popular culture themes
Scissors, laminator or sticky-back plastic

What you do:
This idea focuses on making sets of laminated superhero/popular culture resources. They can be used in a number of different ways but lend themselves particularly for sorting, matching, classifying and counting activities. Look through the comics/paper with the children and, with their help, identify characters that go together, i.e. This might be a family set, or you might cut out a simple story in four to six squares for children to use. Cut out all the characters/shapes and laminate. For the story squares, add a piece of magnetic tape on the back so they can be used on a magnetic board.

You might make links to well-known stories, for example 'Mr Gumpy's Outing' by John Burningham, and create a similar resource – make the boat, house, the animals and Mr Gumpy, or cut the characters from a spare copy of the book. Laminate these, as well as a small photograph of each child, add Velcro/magnetic tape to the back, and children can retell the story for themselves.
Sets can be stored in clear plastic wallets, with a picture and the name written on the front.

Further Possibilities:
Set up a storytelling space in a quiet corner outdoors. Drape a piece of fabric for the roof, add cushions, a magnetic board, several superhero sets, and see how the children utilise the resources. This will help you plan some next steps.
Use for group games – lay pairs of sets face down on the ground – ask the children to choose one, look at the picture, and then find one the other person in the group that has is a matching piece/is part of the same group.
Make themed post-boxes from small tins/boxes, so children can practice posting resources into the matching tin/box.

Superhero Telephone Book

A simple picture book with favourite characters & their telephone numbers

What you need:

A4 ring binder
Stiff paper in different colours
Comics and/or birthday wrapping paper with a variety of popular culture figures and superheroes
Glue, pens, scissors, hole punch
A variety of old telephones (telephone engineers will sometimes have spares to donate)
Sticky back plastic to cover and protect front of book

What you do:

Take time to listen in and find out who the children's favourite characters are. These will often be informed by television programmes, DVD's, story books and comics. The idea is to develop a superhero telephone book with one character per page, with pictures, drawings and a clear telephone number at the top. Children can then 'telephone' the character who they need to help them!

Set out a selection of pictures, characters or logos from the comics/wrapping paper for the children to decorate each page with. You can match the appropriate colour paper to your character – For example, Blue for Batman, Turquoise for Bob the Builder, red for Spiderman etc.

This also makes it easier to add new pages for new characters, which is helpful, as popular culture figures change quickly. Ask the children to write and/or suggest telephone numbers for each different character. It is very interesting to see what sorts of combinations of numbers they come up with!

Choose a bright title with the children for the front, and cover with sticky back plastic to protect. Your new telephone book is now ready to use. Place next to a selection of telephones.

Model for the children how to look through the book, search for a number (you could make it alphabetical with a small copy of the alphabet inside the front cover for children to refer to), dial and have a conversation.

Further possibilities:

Create a Superhero Telephone box (this could also be a place to hang dressing up resources, hats, eye masks etc, and used as a quick changing room!) Place the Superhero Telephone book inside, and a telephone. Decorate the phone booth with artwork, children's mark-making and pictures from comics in order to support further role-play. To learn real telephone numbers, sing them to a favourite tune. Make a Superhero address book. Engage the children in deciding where the characters live, what type of house, cave or tree, and illustrate the book. Send letters and post cards to favourite heroes and characters.

Idea 3

Themed Graphics or Mark-Making Area

What you need:

Photocopy the logos of popular superheroes onto plain paper and provide small clipboards and pencils

Small selection of coloured paper.   Pens & pencils in themed storage pots.

Use stickers on the pots to link to the characters, or cut and stick on pictures from comics

Clean, empty baked-bean tins make ideal pots for pens, and can be painted appropriate colours. It is important to make sure they have no sharp edges.

Selection of small spiral- bound notebooks (often produced for party bags with popular culture figures on front), restaurant notepads, 'post-its'

Blank and pre-printed post-cards & and stickers for stamps

Date and picture stamps and ink pad

Sellotape, scissors, paperclips and staplers

Small cushions for 2-3 chairs that link to the theme

Posters and pictures from comics/magazines displayed on the wall

Space on the wall or board for children to put up their own drawings and pictures

Favourite comic books and stories, changed regularly – displayed in a 'book box', a decorated cardboard box to store small collections of books (from Activity 7 – 'Helping Young Child Learn to Read' Helen Bromley ISBN: 978-1-903670-32-3). Speech bubble sign saying 'Please tidy this area before you leave! Thanks, Spiderman

What you do:

Organise the resources listed above enticingly (into) in a space with room for 3-4 children, with table and chairs. Once the area is set up observe how the children use the space. You may need to add or take away some materials, and discuss with the children what else they might like in the area.

Further Possibilities:

You can duplicate these resources for outdoors and, if you don't have a covered outdoor writing area, organise a range of similar materials in a deep tray, which can easily and quickly be transported and set up outdoors, weather permitting.

A small tent or den could be set up either indoors or out for the graphics area

Make a post box, in order that children can send letter and cards, and celebrate superheroes' Birthdays!

Send Birthday cards to the children from their favourite characters.

Superheroes and Popular Culture

Idea 4

Superhero Knowledge and Understanding of the World Bags

What you need:

Bat Bag

A 'Bat' themed bag (gift bags with string handles work well) containing: Two or three squares of dark fabric for capes; toy mobile telephone; small Underground map, or map of your local area (available from local tourist office or download from maps.google.co.uk); postcards from around the world; miniature non-fiction and/or story books about bats; spring bat toys, (the sort that after a few moments jump up in the air); small notebooks and pens; giant bouncy ball or giant glass marble; toy bat – Ikea does a good one.

Spider Bag

A 'Spider' themed bag containing: a soft ball of wool or string for making spider webs; large and small toy spiders – (Ikea does a large soft toy spider); the story book 'The Very Busy Spider' by Eric Carle; non-fiction book about spiders/mini-beasts; red fabric squares for capes; sunglasses; spiral notebooks and pens; wind-up bug toy;, sticky spider web; gloves and walkie-talkies.

What you do:

Themed bags offer endless possibilities for exploring the area of Knowledge and Understanding of the World, as well as providing exciting opportunities for imaginative role-play. They also offer children an easy way to transport materials, which will appeal to those children exploring a 'transporting' schema. The thinking behind the bags is to offer something familiar and, through this, also offer something new – for example, extending their first interest into an area of science or natural history.

Organise the materials into the bags and either have a special delivery arrive part-way through the session, or introduce during a group time.

Further Possibilities:

It can be useful to duplicate bags, so 2-3 children can explore a similar theme together. This will avoid too much conflict over new materials.

Provide a camera – and ask children to see if they can find and photograph some real mini-beasts

Add different wind-up toys

Wrap up new objects in tissue paper and place inside the bags for children to find

Have a selection of empty bags for children to use during tidy-up time, to transport small toys and objects. Refer to the book 'Mini-beasts and more' - young children investigating the natural world by Ros Garrick 2006 Early Education.

Superhero and Popular Culture Stories

What you need:

Small ready made books with 2-4 pages and coloured paper for immediate illustrations

Roll of lining paper

Photographs of children engaged in superhero play

Comics, scissors, glue and sellotape

Access to a PC, so children can use technology to write and design their books

What you do:

Listen in to children's comments and ideas as they play. You might join the play, but do this with sensitivity – you will be welcomed if you join in a way that 'fits the game'. Record the play in different ways:–video, photographs, writing notes, or by using a digital voice recorder. (From Argos for around £30) Children will usually be very interested to tell their story, if they can then hear themselves played back! Set up the materials listed on a table outdoors and invite children to create their own story books. You can use the roll of lining paper to create a continuous story outdoors – on the ground or along a fence. Children can draw themselves or their characters, add speech bubbles for comments. Facilitating story-making in this way will help to build confidence, so children begin to see themselves as writers and authors. An example of two such stories can be found below.

The Spider Story

Page 1 – "this is Spiderman and he has a spider in his name"

Page 2 – "this spider doesn't need eyes or teeth or a mouth, he's a baddie!"

Page 3 – "this spider is a goodie, he fights the bad spider!"

Page 4 – "the spider comes down from the web when he has grown up"

The Barbie Story

Page 1 – "this is Barbie"

Page 2 – "Barbie has got muscles cos she fights baddies!"

Page 3 – "Barbie goes to ballet"

Further Possibilities:

Make a display of the books, with links to areas of learning.

Enduring story themes can be set up with messy play materials and small world. (See Idea 6)

Builder's Tray adventure with Cornflour Sludge

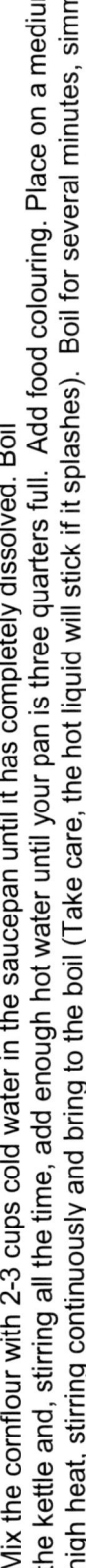

What you need:

Cornflour Sludge

1 large mug cornflour

Large saucepan & wooden spoon

Enough water to almost fill the pan

2 tbsp blue food colouring

1-2 drops essential oil e.g. Lavender (optional)

Selection of small world resources, including superhero figures, leaves, twigs and flowers

Sugar shakers with cornflour, coloured sand,

Aprons

What you do:

Mix the cornflour with 2-3 cups cold water in the saucepan until it has completely dissolved. Boil the kettle and, stirring all the time, add enough hot water until your pan is three quarters full. Add food colouring. Place on a medium-high heat, stirring continuously and bring to the boil (Take care, the hot liquid will stick if it splashes). Boil for several minutes, simmer for 5-10mins. Allow mixture to cool completely before adding essential oil and using. It's a good idea to make the day before, leave overnight in the pan, and you will have a lovely sludgy jelly to play with the next day!

If your sludge is too runny, next time make it with more cornflour.

Put the sludge in a builder's tray or large round washing up bowls. Add a variety of small world/superhero figures, leaves, twigs and flowers, with shakers nearby. Place aprons near the play. Observe the play, and see what else might be added, in response to children's interests.

Further Possibilities:

Hide large chunks of ice with superhero figures frozen inside, and provide small hammers. (Provide eye protector goggles – available from DIY shops)

Add lengths of drainpipe with large buckets and a source of water

Safely site a tape machine with atmospheric watery music, whale sounds etc nearby

Provide sheets of paper for children to add sludge to, with sticks, combs, feathers to make patterns and marks. Add glitter shakers & powder paint.

Laminate photographs of the play characters with names on the back, hang with clothes pegs on string nearby.

Refer to '50 Exciting Ways to Use a Builder's Tray' - Helen Bromley. ISBN: 978-1-903670-15-6, for further recipe ideas.

Idea 7

Superheroes Number Line

What you need:
A5 card, plain or coloured
Dressing up clothes
Face paints (optional)
Laminator & pouches
Felt-tip/marker pen

What you do:
Involve the children in making a number line 1 – 10. Invite them to create their own costumes, paint faces (with parental permission) and maybe make props to suit their character and name badges. Validate any names or suggestions. Beginning with number one, take a photograph of one child. Then photograph two children for number two and so on, up to ten. Photographing outside will give you better light and pictures. Encourage the children to sort themselves into different number groups. Add a clear written number on each card, laminate and display indoors or out using string and clothes pegs. The children can then move the numbers around.

Further Possibilities:
Play physical games – hang individual cards up outside, tell the children to run to a card, until the number of children matches the number of children on each card - make sure you have several cards that add up to the number of children, so that no-one is left out. You could make this more challenging once you have played it a few times, by adding music, and playing in a similar way to musical chairs – in which case, organize number cards, so you have a few children 'spare'.
Display the numbers and ask children to find matching objects in the environment to place by each number, ie. 10 acorns, 3 pebbles, 5 fir-cones, 1 teacher!
Shrink the cards on a photocopier to postcard size, laminate and place in small baskets with the corresponding number of small world objects – dinosaurs, people, mathematical bears etc.
Put a number card in a cloth bag and ask two children to go and collect things in the bag equal to the number.

Idea 8

Alphabet Line

What you need:
A5 card, plain or coloured
Dressing up clothes
Face paints (optional)
Laminator & pouches
Felt-tip/marker pen

What you do:
The idea is to make an A-Z alphabet using children's names and favourite things. Children will be more interested in exploring letter sounds linked to their names and objects they love - B for Barbie and B for Bear will be much more appealing to a child who loves Barbie and has a favourite teddy! Follow the children's lead and invite them to choose objects they like, and explore first letter sounds. Some children might bring special things from home – your alphabet does not need to evolve in any particular order – as it develops, you can say to the children "We need to make a letter 'T' today, who can find something beginning with 'T'? Oh, yes, 'Thomas'!" Etc. If you have two or three children with the same letter beginning their name, they could be photographed together for that letter, or choose other letters that are needed. They may wish to dress up as their favourite characters and be photographed, for example as the letter 'P' for Power Ranger.

Further Possibilities:
Following the children's interests, create more letter cards linked to favourite themes. You might make a set of Power Ranger letters, relating to the colours of the characters. 'R' for the Red Power Ranger, 'B' for the Blue Power Ranger. Photograph children dressed up, or cut pictures from comics to illustrate.
Shrink the finished cards on a photocopier to postcard size, laminate and place in a small basket on a table, where you have stuck down a simple A-Z line. Invite children to match their home-made alphabet to the letters on the table. If space is short, you can set this up on a magnetic wall board, adding a piece of magnetic tape to the back of each letter, or use shoe pockets hanging up, marked with A-Z and ask children to place letter cards in the matching pocket.

Idea 9

Newspaper Hero Stories

What you need:

Books about people who are 'heroes' in the community, for example, Doctors, nurses, Lollipop Lady
Books or posters about famous heroes – Nelson Mandela, Mother Theresa, The Dali Lama, Ghandi,
Amy Johnson, Explorers, Inventors, Sports heroes
Local or National newspaper articles with interesting stories (see examples below)
A 4 Ring Binder

What you do:

One of the ways we can explore the theme of 'heroes' is to introduce real ones. These might be
historical figures, heroes of our time, or stories about people displaying bravery and courage in local
newspapers. You can introduce these to children during group times, and make books available for children to look at when they choose.
It's a good idea to have a mix of different stories, some light and fun, others more serious. Stories with photographs to illustrate them
work well. Collect, laminate and store in a ring binder. It can make a wonderful display for parents to see too.

Suggestions of real newspaper stories that have been collected:

'The Great Hamster Escape' starring Mike, a hamster that survives a recycling plant and is joyfully re-united with his owner!
Children in a South African village playing on a 'play-pump' - looks just like a round-a-bout, but is in fact a water pump collecting water
from underground, storing it in a water tower, providing fresh, clean water for their village.
Boys Dance Troupe- a photograph and story of a group of boys aged 8-9 years old performing a dance they have created for their
assembly.
Local news story about a father who rescues his daughter from a river when she has been washed down a storm drain
Note, make sure you read and check the *content* of stories is appropriate before introducing to the children

Further Possibilities:

Stories can be accessed via News sites on the Internet and displayed on an interactive white board if you have one.
You might link the introduction of a particular hero to a child's or children's interests. For example, children interested in transport may
delight in the story of Amy Johnson who achieved worldwide recognition when, in 1930, she became the first woman to fly solo from
Britain to Australia, flying her Gipsy Moth Plane, "Jason". If you are fortunate to have a Science Museum nearby, you could follow this up
with a trip to see similar aircraft. Encourage children to reflect on their own heroic deeds, for example - when they try something new, do
something they feel scared of, or help a friend.
Children can write their own newspaper articles about events in the setting. This is particularly good when combined with ICT – using the
computer with the children, particularly boys, will encourage their story-making and creativity.
Children's deeds and stories could then be included in the display for parents.

Idea 10

Magic Carpet Ride

What you need:
Large piece of a fabric – a sheet or rag rug. Stretchy Lycra fabric is ideal
Music and CD/tape player

What you do:
Tell the children you are going on a special adventure today, and introduce them to the magic carpet. You may have this hidden in a cloth bag for extra suspense! Spread the 'carpet' out with the children's help and ask them to carefully sit down. (*Some children get completely immersed in the idea of a magic carpet, and forget that the floor underneath is still hard, so do remind them*) Invite them to put imaginary chocolate cake in their pockets for the journey, do up their 'seat belts' and countdown 5 4 3 2 1 for take off! The children can pull the edges of carpet around so they don't fall off. You might play some soft 'flying music', or something more adventurous, i.e. the theme tune to Superman. Describe the flight, 'up we go, into the sky, travelling over the village, mountains, rivers etc, all the way to……… invite the children to suggest where you are going; they will not be short on ideas!

You may have hidden a favourite teddy bear or puppet and have to rescue them, or perhaps you have travelled to the sea-side to eat ice-cream and dance on the beach.

Further Possibilities:
Provide several smaller pieces of fabric for magic carpets, in order that the children can continue with the idea. You could roll these up and wrap them in brown paper, addressed to the children, with a pretend stamp. Perhaps they have been sent as a 'Thank-you' by the teddy whom the children rescued yesterday?! Even better, (if you can) ask a colleague to come in during a group time, saying, 'These have just arrived in the Post…?'
Provide props – simple baskets with pretend food, dressing up clothes, notebooks and pens, rucksacks and bags for children to take on their journeys
Photograph one such journey, ask children for comments, and make into a simple book 'Our Magic Carpet Adventure'.

Superheroes Lycra Dance

What you need:

Large piece of thick lycra – approx 2- 3 m. (*Lycra is not essential; a large sheet will do, though the lycra's stretchiness will add to the sensory experience and excitement! Lycra fabric comes in wonderful colours and different weights, a thicker weight will work better for groups*)

A selection of favourite music including superhero/popular culture themes, e.g. 'Pirates of the Caribbean' music

CD/tape player

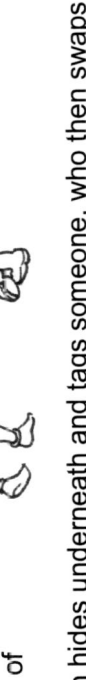

What you do:

The lycra can be used in any of the following ways and, of course, you will discover other games that suit the children you are working with.

Take the lycra outside and fill with leaves and ask your 'superheroes' to bounce the leaves off the lycra as fast as they can.

Add a collection of colourful balloons, or popular culture figures, and bounce until all the resources have been bounced off.

Using music from popular culture themes linked to your children's interests, play a musical statue game – when music plays, move the lycra up and down, or back and forth, and freeze when the music stops.

Double the lycra over, and carefully take turns with one child lying in the middle of the fabric, with an adult and other children gently lifting them.

Superhero tag – group stands in circle holding lycra at waist height. One person hides underneath and tags someone, who then swaps with the person underneath. Make sure the children tag different people to ensure everyone has a turn.

Further Possibilities:

Set off on an imaginary journey by boat, with the children sitting down on the lycra, pulling it up around them. Introduce different music to set the scene. You can also stand in a circle holding the lycra and move it back and forth like a boat on the waves, with an exciting piece of music playing (Pirates of the Caribbean is good). The lycra will make a strong breeze, as you move it up and down, just like being on a boat at sea. Slowly lower the volume of the music to signal the end of the game.

Practice counting altogether as you move the lycra up and down – an exciting and energizing way to count up to large numbers.

Provide two or three smaller pieces of lycra for the children to utilize in self-initiated activities.

Use the large lycra like a giant cloak, and in a large space, run fast holding the lycra above your head – it will stream out behind you and the children can chase after, trying to stay under the cloth!

Idea 12

Woodwork Station

What you need:
A small solid table or woodwork bench, ideally with 2 small vices in order that children can clamp wood
Small wood clamps, saws, hammers, screwdrivers, pliers, screws, nails and sand paper
Different types of wood, in different sizes and shapes – Joinery and carpentry shops will usually have off-cuts to spare
Small bottles of pva glue, and a glue gun, for use under supervision
Masking tape/sellotape. Metal pin clips, large paper clips, string and twine
Lollipop sticks - different sizes and colours
Old chopsticks, kitchen roll tubes, small lengths metal chain, buttons and corks
Old bits of jewellery, large beads, fastenings.
Clipboards and paper, felt-tips, pencils

What you do:
A well-resourced woodwork bench will help children develop small motor skills, and confidence in using a range of tools. Children can be supported to design and make a whole range of different items based on their current interests. In particular, we can encourage children who want to make pretend weapons and guns to be creative, and to use these materials instead of blocks, or Stickle bricks. This supports the play moving from imitative to imaginative.
Safety guidelines about how the tools and materials are to be used, need to be discussed with the children beforehand, and initially a practitioner will need to supervise. You may need to limit the number of children using the station.

Further Possibilities:
Make a poster with the children listing some brief guidelines about how to use the woodwork bench.
Provide a small white board or black board so children who want to use the station can write their names on the list.
Support the process of sustained shared thinking by asking open-ended questions, and making positive comments.
Organise a tool box to store tools safely, or a display board with hooks, with names and outlines of tools.
Provide small stick-on or tie tag labels in order that children can write the names or uses of the different parts of their work
Photograph the children's creations, and include in the Book of Inventions. (See idea 16)

Idea 13

Superhero's Code of Conduct

What you need:

Comics or wrapping paper with children's current popular culture/superhero themes
Felt-tips, crayons, glue sticks, scissors
A4 or A3 card or paper

What you do:

It can be both challenging and exciting when children engage in physical role play. A superhero code of conduct is one way to help children take responsibility for deciding their own, positive rules for energetic play.
Children are deciding what roles to play and the 'story' of their games. 'Pressing a pause button' if feelings begin to run high or conflict develops can be a useful strategy to calm things down, and help children begin to problem solve. A reception class teacher I knew, occasionally videoed this process, in order to help the children see how and why difficulties arose, and what they could do to make the play work better.
Make and decorate a poster of codes and rules to display both indoors and out.

Examples of what some 'codes' might be called:
  'Power Ranger Rules'
  'BEN 10 does it AGAIN!'
  'Spiderman Says'
  'Hide and Seek Code'

Rules might include:
  No real hitting
  Stop if someone gets hurt (call an ambulance to take them to the superhero hospital!)
  Quiet voices inside, loud voices outside
  Fire guns at body, not face

Further Possibilities:

Do a miniature version of the poster to share with interested parents
If there have been difficulties with children being aggressive/physically violent, make a point of 'catching' them being gentle/listening etc and, if possible, photograph and display, or make into a simple book, in order to support behaviour changing. Reward children individually and as a group for creating and following the code, perhaps with a superhero themed picnic?

Idea 14

Giant Superheroes

What you need:

Roll of wallpaper lining
Felt-tips, pens, scissors, masking tape and glue
Paint and rollers
Collage materials, fabric in different sizes and textures, sparkly bits and pieces
Photographs of children's faces, blown up on a photocopier to life size (A4 ordinary print paper is great)

What you do:

Children lie down on a piece of lining paper large enough for their whole body. It helps to tape the paper to the floor, otherwise it keeps rolling up. Draw around the outline of the child – they may want to do a specific 'superhero' pose. Cut out the outline, and provide the materials listed so children can decorate and clothe their figures. It is a very satisfying experience to be able to lie down and create, and indeed this might well be easier and more comfortable for some children. One setting I know sets up their creative materials enticingly on the floor, and even as an adult I felt drawn to lie down and begin exploring.

Further Possibilities:

The figures provide a great display – take photographs of the process and collect quotes from children as they work on their figures.
The photographs, plus quotes written in 'speech bubble' shapes, can then be displayed with and around the figures.

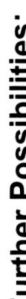

Idea 15

Superhero Characters

What you need:
Paper, card
Crayons or oil pastels
Laminator, though not essential
Small photographs of children's faces

What you do:
Invite children to think up their own superhero characters. Who would they be?
What would they be called? What would their costume be like?
What would their superpower/s be?
Help the children to cut figures from card or stiff paper; draw the costume, and then
colour. Either draw the face, or attach a photograph.
Laminate and hang by strings. It can be very effective to hang the figures up using
fishing twine, which is almost invisible, though children may prefer to use the
characters for games and story-making.

Further Possibilities:
You might arrange the figures (or copies of them) in a circular display, entitled
'circle of friends' as a welcome sign
Add magnetic tape to the back of each figure and stick onto a large magnetic white board. Children can draw the background, and
create stories. Videoing or photographing these stories, then playing them back helps children to review what they have created, and add
appropriate language to describe what's happening. For example, children might describe the story of how their superhero acquired their
power.
The outline of each figure could be drawn onto transparencies, coloured with transparency pens, and used on an overhead projector for
story-telling.

Superheroes and Popular Culture

Book of Inventions

What you need:

A4 photograph album with peel back sheets, so that photographs and captions can be added easily

Junk modelling materials

Tools - scissors, whole punch, staplers, metal joining pins, rulers

Paper, card, masking tape, glue, string, rope etc

Jam-jar lids, wool, collage materials

What you do:

This is a book to collect and display children's creations and inventions. These may occur spontaneously when children access junk modelling materials or you may invite 'invention making' by sending the children a letter asking for their help. For example, 'Dear Power Rangers and Batman, I am sorry to say the three Billy Goats Gruff are stranded on an island, and need to be rescued! Please could you make something to help? Love from or Yours sincerely Mr. Troll'

Provide a selection of materials listed above, and involve the children in coming up with 'inventions' that might help. The inventions can then be photographed, included in the book, with a brief description. Make a title for the front of the album, and cover with sticky-back plastic to protect it.

Further Possibilities:

A copy of the child's invention can be included in their record of achievement (if they have one), and the book can be displayed for parents to see, with information and photographs about the process, and the learning that is taking place.

Introduce children to real inventors and inventions, for example Alexander Graham Bell who invented the telephone. A more recent invention, for example, is how South African Farmers are using bee hive fences to prevent elephants from damaging their crops – the elephants understandably are scared of the ferocious South African bees and will run from a swarm. These can be introduced through short films, books and with parents and practitioners sharing their knowledge.

Read Wendel's Workshop by Chris Riddell (Macmillan Children's Books 2007)

Open-ended role play resources

What you need:

20-30 large squares of lining fabric - available in the local market or fabric shop. One metre of fabric will provide four squares. Lining fabric is usually available in bright colours, cheap and easily washed. The material should not need hemming - the edges stop fraying after several uses. (For babies, make sure any frayed ends are pulled off beforehand.)

Selection of masks, belts, shoes, sunglasses, hats, bags

What you do:

The materials can be incorporated into your environment in a number of different ways. Many boys will prefer to play outdoors, so organizing the resources in a den/cave/selection of large cardboard boxes will invite exploration. You might tie the fabric squares loosely onto a fence or tree, and see what the children do, or set up a tent with the materials attractively laid out inside.

Provide a reading corner with rugs and cushions and books that will stimulate play – Traction Man Is Here by Mini Grey (2005 Red Fox), Max by Bob Graham (2000 Walker Books) or The Magic Bed by John Burningham (2003 Red Fox)

The cloth squares can also be used for movement and dance – encourage the children to hold a square in each hand, stretch high and low, wide and swirling, with large and small arm movements. Using music from popular well-known children's films can be great fun, and particularly useful when working with children with different languages – most children will recognize the tunes and story, even though they do not understand the words.

Further Possibilities:

Use the squares to wrap individual items either for a treasure hunt outdoors, or laid out on a small rug. Items to be wrapped could be, for example, shells, small world figures or animals. (This would suit those children exploring an *enveloping schema*) You might also hide the wrapped parcels into in a 'lucky dip' of paper shredding.

Fill a small suitcase with one of each of a pair of shoes. Hide the other half of each pair in the outdoor area, or in odd places inside the setting and tell the children they have ten minutes to find all the matching shoes and put them together!

Idea 18

Building Base

What you need:

Wheelbarrows, small spades, scoops, rakes, short brooms

Sand, a few bricks, large pebbles and shells

Rope and pulleys

Buckets and containers, tubes and funnels

Large containers – floor standing sandpits, builder's trays, garden containers with handles etc.

Access to water

Good story books – for example:- Billy's Bucket by Kes Gray & Garry Parsons, The Three Little Wolves and the Big Bad Pig by Eugene Trivizas and Helen Oxenbury, The Lighthouse Keepers Lunch, by Ronda and David Armitage

What you do:

These resources provide plenty of opportunities for children to use their strength safely, to lift, carry and create ways to transport materials.

They can be organized on a smaller scale indoors on a large tarpaulin, but ideally work best in the outdoor environment. Set up a building area in one corner where groups of children will be able to play comfortably. Add appropriate signage, including large pictures from comics, (laminate or cover with sticky-back plastic to protect). Bob the Builder characters can also be placed in this area. Make space for the tools to be stored nearby - hooks or clips attached to a wooden board, fastened to a wall, fence, or shed works well. Set up the ropes and pulley systems, one going up and down, and one going horizontally across. Buckets or small bags can then be hung from the hooks to carry sand etc.

Further Possibilities:

Add names and outlines to the tool storage board

Represent some of the ideas from the suggested storybooks, or add your own. For example, for Billy's Bucket you might add lots of different types of buckets with all sorts of sea small-world creatures and real seaweed inside. Children could then write a letter to Billy or draw a picture telling him what they've found in their buckets!

Add peat-free compost and half or whole lengths of drainpipe.

Bury treasure (wrap small plastic cups and/or spoons in silver paper) in the sand

Make giant dinosaur footprints in smoothed sand before children arrive (make templates from cardboard and press into sand). How do the children explain the footprints? How did they get there? Provide a selection of small world dinosaurs.

Idea 19

Target Practice

What you need:

3–4 (cut out) shapes cut from wood/cardboard – for example, a circle, square, triangle and diamond. *They need to be large enough for children to throw beanbags or sponges at.*

Small blackboard and chalk, or a clipboard with paper and pen

Bean bags, sponges, balls

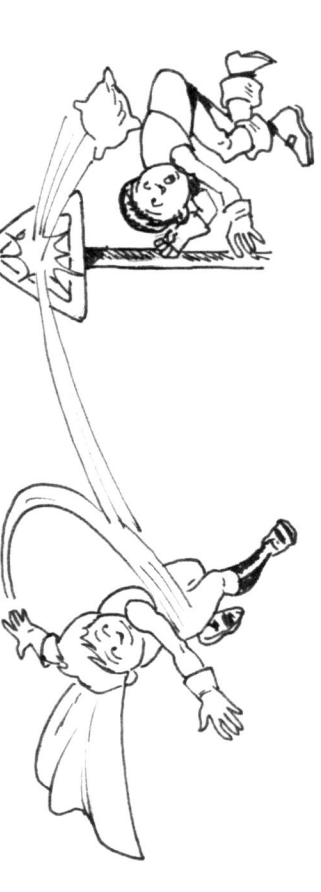

What you do:

Paint the shapes different colours – you might include a 'bulls-eye' in the middle. Varnish, or seal with a thin coat of PVA glue. Allow to dry, then set the targets up against a fence or wall or shed. Wooden targets can be screwed firmly to a solid surface. Set the targets up away from a through-fare, or plan a specific throwing time.

Put the beanbags/sponges/balls into buckets for easy transportation. It can be useful to mark a throwing line on the ground with chalk to stand behind - with practice the line can be moved further away. You can support children to throw both over-arm and under, and to count how many 'bulls-eyes' they score. A record of scores can be kept on a nearby blackboard.

Further Possibilities:

You might develop a points system, with the bulls-eye scoring a higher amount than the rest of the target, and involve children in adding up their scores.

The targets could link to other interests, for example, monster shapes or modes of transport – a plane, bus, train or car. Include the Target game as part of a superhero special assault course (see idea 37).

Instead of Targets, hang up a large fabric sheet or piece of lining paper, and throw sponges loaded with paint. With children's help, paint and label boxes Rather than a flat target, you might also make targets out of different size cardboard boxes. With children's help, paint and label boxes 'small box', 'tall box', 'wide box' etc. or theme each box with a different superhero character and decorate accordingly!

These activities will appeal to children exploring a trajectory schema – up and down or back and forth movements. Re-directing a dynamic schema pattern creatively will enable children to continue their exploration in a way that works for practitioners and parents.

© Lawrence Educational   Superheroes and Popular Culture

Idea 20

Superhero Signs

What you need:

A selection of large brightly coloured 'sale' or 'special offer' signs
blank pre-cut cards available from stationery shops, or cut shapes you need from coloured card.
('blank explosion' signs can be found on the Times Educational Supplement website, register for free to access teacher resources,
articles, forums – http://www.tes.co.uk)
Felt-tip pens/pencils/crayons

What you do:

These signs can be used in many different ways, for example:
Set up a selection of pre-cut signs together with felt-tip pens or crayons on a table to encourage mark-making. You might also add comics, scissors, glue, collage materials.
They could be made into badges, or displayed hanging up as 'superhero stars'.
Write children's names on the signs.
Create greetings in different languages – wonderful to ask parents to stay and help with this, particularly Dads.
Label artwork, inventions, models with the signs.
Make large signs or 'explosions' on the wall with 'made-up' sound words - 'Kerpluuuunk!' 'Booosh!' 'shesammmm!' etc – listen in when children are playing physical games, especially those that include mock fighting and see if there are particular sounds they use – this is a fun way to play with phonics and model how to write down letter sounds.

Further Possibilities:

Create a simple story on a notice board with the children. Decorate the background, add figures, characters that the children have created and use the 'superhero signs' to narrate the story. Invite the children to suggest wording, and encourage them to write their own signs. Scribe signs for children who need help.
Send messages on the signs to different teachers and other children, asking children to be the delivery person.
Make giant medallions – make a hole at one side and provide glitter, glue, sequins, sparkly trimmings. Encourage children to add whatever they like using lots of glue, allow to dry and you will have some very impressive jewellery!

Idea 21

Tree Register

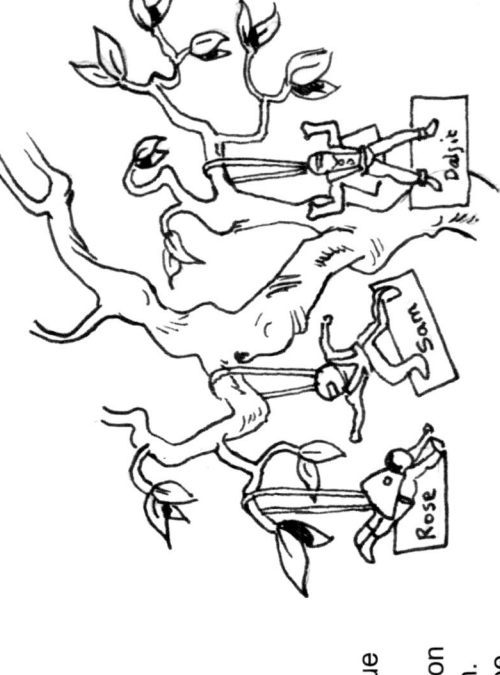

What you need:

Real tree branches or a small tree shape, cut from paper or card
Stiff paper
Sticky back Velcro strips
Thread or thin ribbon
A small name label for each child
Laminator
Sticky-back plastic
Pens, felt-tips, crayons

What you do:

Paint the tree branches or the card/paper tree. A watered down coat of PVA glue will seal and protect the painted surface. Place the branches in a heavy based pot with pebbles or sand and put on a table or wide shelf. Stick the paper tree on the wall or notice board. Both trees need to be within easy reach of the children. Add painted leaves, or make lots of handprints, cut them out, and add to the tree for 'leaves'.

Cut out small superhero figures of the same size, for all the children to have their own to decorate, and add their name label to the front. Laminate or protect each figure with sticky-back plastic, and add a small piece of Velcro to the back, with the corresponding piece stuck to the paper tree. Add a loop of thread or ribbon to the figures for the 'branches' tree, so the children can hang them up. Children can find their figure each day and put it on the tree as part of a self-registering game.

Further Possibilities:

Ask the children for ideas for a title for the tree – 'who's here today?' perhaps?
You might use the figures to decide where children sit for lunch.
You might use the figures to develop games during small group times.

Idea 22

Super Beat Baby

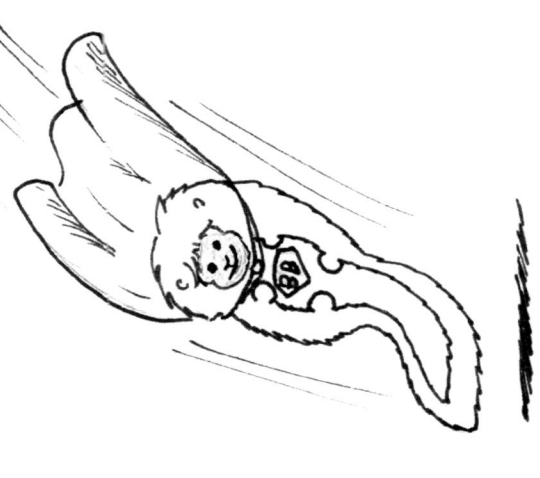

What you need:
A Beat Baby or small teddy
Fabric scraps, string or ribbon
Small box and lid, or mini-suitcase

What you do:
This idea came from a superheroes workshop where one practitioner created a mini cape and crown for a silver 'going-home' beat baby. Super Baby was born! Beat Babies® are small furry creatures that curl up into a ball, small enough to fit in one's hand. I have found them to be very useful props for storytelling and for supporting personal, social and emotional development. Make a cape and cap for your Beat Baby or teddy with the children and ask them to suggest what superpowers the Super Baby might have? Ask the children to make a den for the Super Baby, and to think of some special missions or adventures for the Super Baby to go on. Provide a small box or mini-suitcase so the children can help Super Baby pack.

Further Possibilities:
Send a coded message from Beat Baby Headquarters saying there is an emergency, e.g. the bird feeder is empty, and Super Baby's help is needed to fill it up.
Discuss with the children ways that Super Beat Baby might help them with things they found difficult.
Super Baby could go home with the suitcase to each child's house for a special weekend, (add a small disposable camera, so the child's family can take a picture). The child could add a small item from home to the suitcase.

Beat Baby® is a registered trademark of Lawrence/Bayley.
Beat Babies are available in six different colours from Lawrence Educational.

The Bat Cave

What you need:

Where possible, theme the following resources to link with children's interests, i.e. 'Spiderman' cushions, blue pen pots, notebooks with pirate pictures on the front cover, a duvet or fabric linked to a favourite popular culture figure.

Clothes pegs, lengths of different sorts of fabric

Small roll of bamboo/reed fencing, string, masking tape

Rag rug, cushions and/or a few chairs

Sturdy tape machine, story and song tapes, telephones

Doctor's or first-aid kit

Small notebooks and pens

Story books

Large tape measure, pen, paper and clipboard, small paper tape measures

What you do:

Dens that children are involved in designing and making will usually last longer and will be more successful. Gather all the materials and any other props you think appropriate, and discuss with the children the best place for the den. (Base some of your suggestions on the children's preferred play spaces). Demonstrating how to use the tape measure, measure the lengths of cloth, make marks, and record some of the measurements. (Have plenty of paper and tape measures for the children to use) Build a structure together using the string, large pieces of fabric, clothes pegs and the roll of bamboo fencing. Put the rag rug inside, along with the remainder of the resources.

Further Possibilities:

Plan for some children to be in the den at snack time.

Ask the children to write some signs for the den, for example 'Supers Only!' 'No Dinosaurs in the Den!'

Take time to read stories to small groups, or one or two children in the den.

Provide a basket with a selection of wigs and role play resources.

Idea 24

Gun Licence

What you need:
Blank postcards or small pieces of cut-out plain card
Pens, colouring pencils
Laminator and pouches

What you do:
One of the issues that can arise when children play games with home-made weapons/guns is how to set reasonable and appropriate limits. This is a fun and contextual way to do so.
Print on the cards the words 'GUN SAFETY LICENCE' followed by: NAME; DATE OF BIRTH; DATE OF LICENCE; SIGNATURE with space provided for the information to be inserted. Leave a small blank square space for a photograph or drawing of the child. Ask children to fill in the details and decorate the licence.
Take time to discuss simple rules with the children about keeping everyone safe and happy. It is important that children who don't usually engage in this type of play are included in the discussion, to facilitate communication between different groups. Two or three simple rules are plenty and, where possible, voice the rules in the positive. For example:-
Say what you do want, rather than what you don't. - 'Point guns away from faces', 'Gun-play outdoors', 'Stop the game if someone gets hurt' etc.
Print and copy the rules and stick or write them on the back of each license that you issue. These rules will also inform your policy about this type of play. (*See the sample policy for superhero/weapon play in the back of this book*). If a child break the rules, you can then remind them of their earlier agreement to follow them when engaged in this type of play.

Further possibilities:
The licences will last longer if you laminate them, and can be stored in a special, decorated gun license shoe box. Punch a hole in the corner of the licence, so it can be attached to a belt loop via a key chain. These can usually be bought cheaply in £1 shops.
Make a point of showing your appreciation of children who stick to the rules and take care of each other.
This could in turn develop into 'Certificates of Merit' or 'Badge of Honour Awards', where you celebrate children who have really thought about and practiced safe play. Make some simple certificates to give out.
Write a story about the children who engage in this play – illustrate it simply using photographs of the play in action, and read it to them at group time. This will encourage the children to see themselves as story-makers, and invite them to write their own stories.

Giant Spider Web

What you need:

Large ball of soft wool, or thick string (thin wool or string can get too tight around little fingers or wrists)

Props – A large soft toy spider is ideal and a selection of teddies

What you do:

Sit everyone in a large circle, and show the children the ball of wool. Make a small loop in the end of the wool and ask one child to hold on to it. You can then begin to weave the wool across the circle, giving each person their own piece of wool to hold until everyone is holding a piece, finishing with yourself so you have the remainder of the ball. You will then have a giant spider web in the middle!

Another way to do this is to give the ball of wool to one person, ask them to hold tight to the end and choose someone to throw the ball of wool to! That person then holds a piece and throws the ball to someone else, and so on, until the wool has gone all around the group, finishing with yourself.

You can introduce your spider who comes to visit the web to say hello to everyone (be aware that some people might be scared of spiders!) or introduce other animals. A good song is

> *Upon a spider's web one day*
> *One little spider went out to play*
> *Upon a spider's web one day*
> *He/They found it such enormous fun*
> *That he asked another little friend to come!*

Finish the game by winding up the wool, counting as you go.

Further Possibilities:

Leave out some small balls of similar wool and see what the children do with them.

Make a giant spider's web outside, between trees, bushes or fencing. Make some spiders with fluffy pipe cleaners to live on the web!

Introduce some good spider story books, (The Very Busy Spider by Eric Carle is good Puffin 1996 ISBN-10: 0241135907) and a selection of non-fiction books about spiders/mini beasts.

Create some spider web wrist cuffs by winding a small amount of wool around sections of kitchen roll tube – for the children who enjoy being Spiderman!

Involve the children in a papier-mâché project to make a giant spider or bug, with 'wild' eyes and long legs (*you might look at the sculptures of Louise Bourgeois for inspiration.*)

Idea 26

Popular Culture Story Tree

What you need:
A tree or branches set into a large container indoors or outdoors.
Strips of calico and light fabric
Felt-tips, pens

What you do:
This is an alternative way to create stories. The stories can be made from pictures, prints, writing or a combination. Provide lengths of fabric, about 40cm X 10cm, with a selection of pens and felt-tips. Ask children to think of a story they might like to share with the garden animals. These may centre on popular culture or not. Then help the children to tie their stories on the Story Tree. You might also add some decorations and tinsel.

If carrying out this activity outside it is a really good idea to put together an 'Authors and Illustrators Toolkit' (as suggested in Activity 1 of 'Literacy Outdoors' - Lawrence Educational – ISBN: 978-1-903670-53-8)

This might contain:
A plastic toolbox with a handle.
Pens, post it notes, string, sellotape, envelopes, postcards, writing paper, scissors, spiral bound notebooks, etc.

Further Possibilities:
Instead of stories, children might like to make wishes to hang up, or special messages.
Using twigs, willow and grasses, you might work together to weave figures to sit in the tree.
String outdoor fairy lights on the tree for the winter months.

Idea 27

Superhero Treasure Boxes

What you need:

A variety of natural materials to provide fascination and a rich sensory experience, such as:

Shells of different shapes, texture and colour

Black, polished pebbles – available from garden centres

Lengths of hessian or cotton rope in different diameters.

Lengths of chain with sealed links in different gauges

Satin and velvet ribbons in bright colours

Interesting brooches, bangles and necklaces

Piece of unusual driftwood

A large gemstone or crystal (make sure it has no sharp edges)

Sparkly sequined scarf

Kaleidoscope

Giant marbles

Metal scoop

Bead bag, or purse, small metal candlesticks, giant wooden or bone buttons

What you do:

Collect any of the suggestions above, and add your own objects, based on the children's interests into a large basket or box with lid. You could put a tiny round sticker on each object – then everyone will soon learn that anything with a blue sticker, for example, lives in the treasure box. Explore the basket with small groups and invite them to bring their own special objects to join the treasure! Children can then use the treasure to expand on their imaginative games, perhaps adding the objects and materials to block play, or small world.

Further Possibilities:

Plan a treasure hunt, where children can go into the outdoor space to find whatever 'treasure' takes their fancy, perhaps 'magic' sticks that link to a favourite story etc.

Invite children to create living pictures with the materials – you can provide a large piece of card or paper for background, and then photograph the pictures, before the treasure is re-used, or replaced in the basket.

You might play 'feely bag' games, where one child feels an object in the bag, and has to guess what it is, or describe it in a small group, or 'what's on the tray', where you remove one object at a time, and children have to guess which one is gone!

Idea 28

Super Story Bag

What you need:
A selection of good story books - you can find a list of recommended superhero stories for young children here:
http://www.amazon.com/super-hero-stories/
Other themed story bags might include space travel, wild animals or pirates
A blue and other coloured fabric drawstring bags
Either a pre-recorded tape to go with the story or make your own (this is a great way to involve parents and families)
Props to suit your story and a simple home-made game

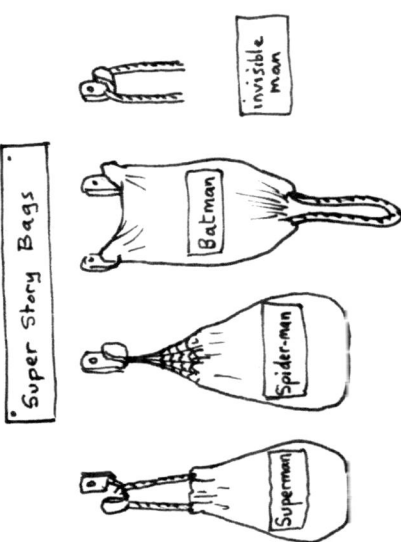

What you do:
Decide on your story and gather props and resources together for your story bag. You will need to have duplicate copies of books, one for the setting and one for your story bag. I have included a recipe below to make a Super Story Bag for 'Max' by Bob Graham.

'Max' is a gentle story about a little boy with superhero parents. He is struggling to learn how to fly and to deal with bullies at school.....but discovers a small deed can make him a hero just the same.

In a blue fabric bag include:
A copy of the book and ask a Dad or male colleague to narrate the story onto a short running tape
A length of red fabric, black eye mask, a pair of red gloves
Small model jet airplane and a soft toy bird (the RSPB make birds with real life bird calls, which make a sound when bird is squeezed)
5-6 small laminated cards linked to the story – an easy way to do this is to minimize and photocopy (being aware of copyright) some of the important pages, with a small amount of text from the book. Children can then order these cards into the right sequence and practice recognizing key words of the story.
Make a simple domino game with main images: - 'Max', the bird, grandma, grandad and the airplane. Place in a plastic wallet to keep together.
Title the story bag, and attach a laminated list of the resources enclosed, with a polite request - 'Max says please look after this bag!'

Further Possibilities:
The bag can be borrowed to support families playing and reading together.
Play a simple game "Max says......" just like "Simon says...." but include in the game some of the things Max does in the story.
Invite grandparents into the setting to read and tell stories. You might ask them about heroic deeds they did in the past.

Idea 29

The Superhero Band

What you need:

Empty water bottles in different sizes
Paper plates
Large elastic bands
Empty tissue boxes
Staplers, tape, glue, ribbons, string, crepe paper, paint, stickers, labels, rice,
dried peas, beads, glitter, sparkles, sequins.
Short lengths of wooden dowling rod and large curtain rings or bells, felt-tips,
Tins – round biscuit tins or SMA milk tins
Pictures of children dressed up, printed on paper, sticky back plastic

What you do:

All the resources listed above can be used to make a variety of simple musical instruments:
Remove labels from bottles and fill with a mixed handful of the rice/peas/beads/glitter and sparkly bits. Glue the lids on and invite the
children to stick stickers, pictures, painted labels on the outside. Ask the children to choose coloured ribbons/string to tie around the neck
of the bottles.
Place a small handful of rice/lentils in the middle of one plate, lay another on top and staple the edges together, being careful not to lose
all the filling. Tape up the edges and over the ends of the staples. Paint both sides of the paper shaker, add glitter and stickers. Attach
some long streamers made from crepe paper.
Tape round edges of tins, and decorate the outside (but not bottom of tin) with photographs of children dressed up, cover with sticky back
plastic for the drums
Drill a hole ½ inch from one end of the dowling rods. Thread 3-4 curtain rings or bells with onto ribbon, tie through the hole and knot
securely for shaking sticks. Write or draw on the sticks.
Finally, make quick guitars with the elastic bands stretched across the hole part on the tissue boxes, for children to strum. Decorate
boxes as children wish.

Further Possibilities:

Invite parents to a superhero band performance, accompanying well-loved songs.
Play along to a superhero theme tune, or piece of classical music.

Idea 30

Drawing to Music

What you need:

Large sheets of sugar paper

Large crayons in different colours

Music CD's with a varied selection of music – link to favourite heroes and popular culture - Libraries usually have good music sections, in particular CD's of recent popular films. Disney films are generally a great source of wonderful music.

What you do:

Choose a selection of different music to play: fast and lively, classical, slow and soft, dramatic and scary.

Make a space on the floor where children can lie down comfortably on their tummies. Ask them to choose two different crayons, and to begin to draw when they hear the music start. Encourage them to use the whole of the paper space, and draw in response to the different music.

Play short sections of music one after the other – do not direct the children what to draw as the whole idea of this activity is for children to draw with complete freedom. When the music stops, invite the children to think of a title for their piece, and then team up with a partner and tell them about their drawing.

This is a useful opportunity to find out what themes and interests are current for the children in your setting.

Further Possibilities:

Create a display of drawings and photographs for parents, with a list of music.

Provide lengths of coloured ribbon or dancing cloths and invite the children to move and dance to some of the music.

Introduce any family, friends, colleagues into the setting to play an instrument or perform a dance and investigate local theatres/schools for potential dance/music performances to attend.

One reception class teacher I know has developed a Power Rangers 'Write Dance' sequence together with her class.

Write Dance: A Progressive Music and Movement Programme for the Development of Pre-writing and Writing Skills in Children (Paperback) by Ragnhild Oussoren Voors.

© Lawrence Educational   Superheroes and Popular Culture

Idea 31

Superhero Squirt Bottles

What you need:

Clean empty shampoo bottles
Cheap plastic shower curtain
Runny paint or coloured water
Paper or large squares of card
String and wooden post
Paint aprons

What you do:

Ask parents to donate empty shampoo bottles. With aprons on, mix up watery paint or coloured water solutions with the children and fill the bottles with it. Protect surfaces, either the floor or a vertical space like an outside wall, with the shower curtain. Stick large sheets of paper/card onto the surface, and squirt away! Encourage the children to experiment with patterns, colours and shapes.

Encourage the children to choose colours for the squirt bottles, linked to their superheroes, for example, 'Spiderman Red', 'Thomas Blue', 'Percy Green'. You might then use the large sheets of artwork for a display, with photographs of the 'process' in action, then invite the children to create stories or comments 'I like Spiderman because....'

Further Possibilities:

Hammer the wooden post into the ground and spread paper on the floor/ground all around it. Make a smallish hole in the lid of either a shampoo bottle or water bottle, fill with the watery paint, and then tie firmly upside down to the post with the string – it will help the bottle stay secure if you make a groove in the top of the post for the string to sit into.

Swing the bottle around the post and watch the paint spray out, or swing it back and forth to see what sort of pattern develops. Alternatively, run the wheels on wheeled toys through muddy puddles or through the watery paint mixture, and invite the children to cycle back and forth across large sheets of paper on the outdoor surface. Some wonderful patterns will appear.

Idea 32

Create a Comic Book Story

What you need:

Digital Camera

Access to power point program on a PC

Costumes and role play resources

Face paints

What you do:

Introduce and read some stories from comics to the children, taking time to discuss who the characters are and what happens to them.

Invite your children to suggest ideas for a very simple story, with a beginning, middle and end. Ask the children to choose which character they will be, how they might like to dress up, make a costume, and with parents' permission, paint their faces to help create their character.

You can use a simple pro-forma on an A4 sheet to help the children decide the beginning, middle and end of their story. This is a wonderful way to model basic story structure and involve the children in creating their own special story!

Take some photographs of the story, - children dressed up, interacting etc. and then use these to illustrate the three scenes. Download the photographs together with the children, and cut and paste them into a power point presentation – these are very easy to use and most programs have a power point wizard to help you. It would be a good idea to familiarize yourself with a power point program before doing the activity with the children. Once you get going there are all sorts of wonderful things you can, for example sound effects and music! Once the photographs are in sequence, ask the children to decide simple captions for each picture. Print the power point off as 'hand-outs', 2 slides per page, and, voila, your comic strip story is done!

Further Possibilities:

Create other comic book stories based on children's real experiences in the setting. You can then show a power point comic strip story to the whole group.

Make a comic by also including any of the following: - a recipe, games e.g. mazes, spot the difference and join the dots, a photograph page for children to 'send-in' pictures of themselves dressed as their favourite characters etc.

Based on the work of 'Vivian Gussin Paley', set up a story-telling 'stage'. Tape a small oblong space on the floor with masking tape and ask the children to sit around the edge. Tell a very short story, based on some of the children's interests. Then invite suggestions for another short story. Ask one child to tell their story and write it down, word for word. Then ask for volunteers to act the story. The child who has suggested the story helps to 'direct', so encourage them to tell the 'actors' where to stand, what to do, and act the story out in words and actions. Initially, keep this technique short but, as the children develop confidence, you will be able to do more than one story.

More information on this can be found at www.makebelievearts.co.uk

Idea 33

Superhero Mobiles

What you need:

Hoops (the sort you spin around your waist)
Lollipop sticks or sticks for the garden.
String, glue, scissors, wool, masking tape, fabric pieces and collage – buttons, sparkles, eyes etc.

What you do:

Set up two work stations, one for decorating the hoop and another for making different characters to hang onto it. The idea is to have a chandelier-like shape to hang your mobile figures from.

Tape one end of a long strip of fabric to the hoop and begin to wrap it tightly round, so the plastic surface of the hoop is completely covered. This works best if you use a mix of different fabrics in bright patterns and colours. Tape the end firmly in place. Tie one end of three pieces of ribbon or string onto the hoop, equal distance apart, then tie the other three ends together so the hoop can be hung up. Create different popular culture figures with the children. Help the children to tie the sticks together, and begin to wrap fabric pieces around the figures to dress them, rather like giant 'worry dolls' – they can add collage materials, a face and hair etc. Attach a piece of string to the top of each character and tie them onto the hoop – they look good if fastened at different heights. If the sticks prove too difficult to work with, make some figures from cardboard for painting and sticking

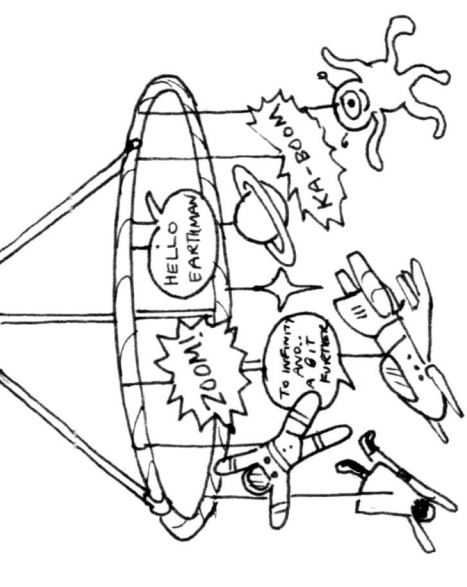

Further Possibilities:

Provide large tie-on luggage labels and scribe children's comments, or ask them to make suggestions of things their characters might say. Tie the labels onto the hoop, in between the different characters.

You might theme the mobiles to link into celebrations and festivals, for example, add dragons or animals from the Chinese Zodiac to celebrate New Year.

You might limit the colour theme to just black and white, and also add materials, such as chimes and bells to make sounds as the mobile moves in the wind.

Idea 34

Stunt Fighting Choreography

What you need:

A clear space, either indoors or out. An adult who is willing to spend time working together with the children to support them in finding safe ways to act out physical play and fighting movements

What you do:
Rationale-

Stunt people and martial arts specialists work hard to perfect movements and make scenes appear effortless and REAL. Children may well believe the physical feats of daring *are real*, and will want to emulate their heroes. Boys will have a need to test their strength, physical power and control, and helping them find ways to engage in safe rough and tumble play and pretend fighting is an appropriate way to support this. With sensitivity, we can engage with children's curiosity and pose open-ended questions - 'if there was a real fire, and we didn't have Mr. Freeze to turn everything to ice, what could we do instead?' We can build their awareness of the differences between fact and fantasy without doing away with the importance of having heroes in our lives.

There will also be instances where children have witnessed real or televised film violence, and this will undoubtedly be acted out through play. Redirecting a child's need to express their experiences will be more healthy than trying to stop it altogether, and offers them a different, more loving view of the world – where it is not right to hurt people, or to be rough with their friends. Encouraging children to make noises to go with movements will help safe expression of feelings.

There are two rules to stunt fighting - no real hitting, and stop if someone says STOP! Work collaboratively with the children to create simple fight moves - pretending to throw a punch and clapping your hands loudly for the 'hitting' sound is very effective! Being the person who has been 'hit' and reeling backwards holding your nose is also good. Kicks and spins, with cat like noises work well. You lose a point if you accidentally touch anyone!

Further Possibilities:

Be clear there is a time and place for stunt fighting, i.e. Not just before lunch, or as children are leaving the setting.
Clearly label it as such – 'Stunt Fighting', which makes it easier to ask 'is this real fighting or stunt fighting?'. Real fighting tends to be clumsy, less coordinated and quieter.
You might try adding music – The Japanese Kudu drummers, 'Stomp' or film music, 'Crouching Tiger, Hidden Dragon' would all work well.

Idea 35

The Movement Space

What you need:

A space - away from quiet play areas or walk-ways

Soft mats to provide a padded surface for rolling, bouncing, etc

Large firm cushions and, if possible, some soft play equipment – cylinders, triangles, seats, though these are in no way essential

Some lengths of fabric in a basket

A few cardboard boxes – these can be stored flat when not in use.

Some resources linked to the popular themes or super heroes your children are interested in.

What you do:

The idea is to provide a safe, contained space for physical play. For many settings, space will be at a premium, so the movement corner will have to take turns with other activities. With this in mind, it would be useful to have an 'OPEN' and 'SHUT' sign for when the space is available (or not), and for it to be 'OPEN' at the same time each day. An introductory session with the children to discuss how to use the space would be useful. Possible questions to ask: Is there too much in it? What else might you like? Are there enough pieces of fabric? Do we need pictures on the wall? What sort of games could we play here?

You might need to limit numbers to begin with – a small blackboard or other surface to write down children's names. Perhaps have some stickers available, so that once a child has had a turn, a sticker is placed next to their name?

Further Possibilities:

Theme the space – for example, turn the space into a wild jungle. Hang green crepe paper from the ceiling, make giant grasses to stick to the wall, a tiger peering from behind..... find some jungle night sounds, big cats howling, and play the CD quietly Or turn it into Aladdin's Market, with bright sparkly fabric hanging up, large baskets to hide in. Posters and pictures of market scenes, provide some Ali Baba hats, pretend snakes, and some magic lamps.

Idea 36

Superhero Speech Bubbles

What you need:
Pieces of card cut out in the shape of speech bubbles
Large felt-tip pens

What you do:
Have a talk with the children about the sorts of things superheroes do. Are there particular things that certain heroes do? For example, if you were 'Super-Cat' would you purr very loudly, jump very high, and rescue birds who get stuck in the garden?!

This can lead into conversations about 'If I was a superhero I would..........'

And then ask the children to write down on the speech bubble cards, what *they would do*. These can make a welcoming display for visitors into the setting. Scribe for those that need it.

Just a word of caution..... Some children may be dealing with difficult and challenging experiences at home. In some cases we may inadvertently stumble upon a disclosure when we least expect it. You will, of course, be guided by your child protection procedure and take care to respond sensitively and with open questions.

Further Possibilities:
You might keep the comments simple - about things children like to do in the setting.
Turn a small selection of speech bubbles into questions to ask the group......How many songs have we sung?
How many books have we read today? How many songs have we sung?
How much lunch can you eat today?

Idea 37

Superhero Assault Course

What you need:

A variety of physical play equipment, both bought and home-made – old tyres (garages usually pleased to donate)
Cardboard boxes, planks and bricks, a tunnel, large plastic flower pots, bean bags, space hopper, hollow barrel, rope, A frame, slide attached, hoops to roll.

What you do:

The idea is to set up a physically challenging assault cause based on children's abilities. Children need to develop their gross motor muscles before their small motor muscle groups, thus lots of running, balancing, climbing, throwing, swinging, hopping etc will help them to develop co-ordination, accuracy and physical strength. Try and think of as many different activities, organized close together, which challenge the children to do a range of different movements.

For example, lay out the tyres in pairs (great to have about 10) so children have to put 1 foot in the middle of each tyre and run along. Put the bean bags in one flower pot and move the other a distance away. Children have to use their head/shoulders/top of their feet, etc to transport them but they are not allowed to touch the bean bags with their hands!

They have to go through the tunnel on their front (if this is too easy, can they go through on their backs?)

They must balance along a length of rope laid on the ground and not 'fall-off', and/or balance along a narrow plank set on top of two bricks.

They must run up the slide and jump from the top, land on a mat, hop on the space hopper etc.

Further Possibilities:

Have a competition between teachers and children!

Hide treasure around the course.

Time each person with a stop-watch.

Try some of the games blind-fold, being led by a partner.

Ask the children to plan the course and devise some new games.

Idea 38

Popular Culture Bingo

What you need:

Comics, wrapping paper or print-offs from the internet of super hero characters.
A4 card, glue, pens, paper, scissors, sticky-back plastic

What you do:

Depending on the ages and stages of the children you could use pictures only, or pictures and words together. A good idea is to begin with pictures and add words once the children are confident playing the game.

Mark out 4-6 equal squares on your pieces of card. Stick a picture of a character in each square. You will need to print (or photocopy) multiple copies of the same, and have a duplicate set for hiding, or 'calling'. Leave room in each square for the children to place a tick or mark.

Cover the cards with sticky-back plastic to protect them. They can be used over and over again - make sure the pens you give children to mark them with are water based, not permanent. Mount the duplicate set of figures onto individual pieces of card, and cover with sticky-back plastic.

They can be used in different ways:
Hide the individual cards in different places and ask the children to look for each one. They can then tick off the corresponding picture on their 'bingo' card. You will need to model for them how the game works initially.
Give each child in a small group a bingo card, place the *individual* cards face down in the middle, and take turns to turn them over one at a time. The children can practice spotting and ticking off the pictures!

Further Possibilities:

Instead of individual *pictures*, make individual *word* cards that correspond to the 4-6 characters. Children can then begin to match the words, with your help, to their pictures. They will be very interested to see their favourite character's names written down. You can then begin to do themed bingo games, e.g. Bugs and mini-beasts, Dinosaurs, Teachers in the setting etc.

Popular Culture Dominos

What you need:

Comics, wrapping paper or print-offs from the internet.
Sites like: http://www.bbc.co.uk/cbeebies/colour/, allow you to print off images of popular characters.
A4 card, glue, pens, paper, scissors, sticky-back plastic

What you do:

In a similar way to the bingo idea print off or copy popular culture characters but, this time, stick (only two) one picture onto either end of a small length of card measuring about 4cm x 12cm. (make them bigger if you wish – in particular bear in mind the needs of partially sighted children). Make sure you have a good selection, but not too many – the children will not choose to play the game if it is too complicated.

You may find you need to add more dominos as you go along. Indeed, every so often add a couple of new characters, or even old ones depicted in a different way, to keep the game interesting and up to date! You can include some blank domino cards that can be used for any character. (These could be Mr. Invisible!)

Further Possibilities:

For alternative dominos, use small photographs of favourite toys and play resources in your setting instead of popular culture characters.
Use some 'word' dominos, and practice matching words to the characters or pictures.
Bring 'real' dominos for the children to play with. The most fun of all is to set them up just close enough to touch, and see if you can make them all fall down!
There are some wonderful videos of domino world records on 'You Tube', but obviously check they are suitable before showing.

A Hero's Medal

Idea 40

What you need:
Card, pens, scissors, glitzy paper – gold or silver, red ribbon, stick-on gems

What you do:
The idea is to make large medals or certificates, rather like Head Teachers Awards, which can be awarded for acts of bravery, courage, helpfulness and hard work. It is important to keep a record of who has received an award, when and what for, and to make sure that each child receives at least one. Children will have their individual strengths and, what is easy for one child may well be extremely difficult for another, so effort and perseverance must be taken into account. The awards work best if they are given sparingly. An awards ceremony during group time is great fun, and you might introduce the award with some special superhero music – The Superman theme tune would be great!

Choose your title to suit - 'Gold Award', 'Amazing Achievement', 'Captain Incredible does it again!' The medals can be made of circles of card (jam jar lids could be used as a base too) and then covered in silver/gold paper. Leave space to add a sticker with a title, name, date and reason for the award. Add stick-on gems and thread onto red ribbon. It is worth making a stock of them to have to hand. Put a grand title, and leave space to write the child's name, and what the award is for.

Certificates can be designed on a computer or printed by hand.

Further Possibilities:
Provide pens and small pieces of card, and invite the children to create their own awards and medals to give to each other, or the puppets in the setting.

Award a special medal to an adult in the setting occasionally, sharing with the children why it has been awarded, and including them in the ceremony.

You might use the medals and certificates collectively and award a small group for some excellent behaviour, or particular kindness. This will support group bonding and team-building.

You might also create another type of reward system for particular activities, using superhero stickers on a name chart, and when the whole group has collected a certain number, have a special treat, ice-cream/a picnic/video.

Superhero Hideways

N.B. Before carrying out this activity ensure that all the necessary risk assessments have been completed. You may need to visit beforehand to check suitability, and discuss with local council/park-keeper that it is alright to build dens/camps

What you need:

A nearby park or wood.
Books or pictures of dens and camps.
String, snacks and drinks, camera.
Superhero characters.
And the usual things you might take for an outing, e.g. First aid kit

What you do:

Plan a trip to the park or woods - invite parent volunteers, so there is a good adult to child ratio.
The children can carry small rucksacks containing string, and a drink and snack. Consult some books and pictures of dens and camps, to provide inspiration. It is fun to make one big den with everyone helping to carry sticks and lengths of wood and finding branches with leaves for the roof. Or put a piece of string up between two trees and drape fabric over to make a make-shift tent. You could use some large branches for seats, or take a plastic backed picnic blanket. Then have your snacks inside.

This activity involves children working together to create something, using their strength and problem solving skills.

Further Possibilities:

If the outdoor space is private, and you have permission, a small, safe bonfire can be a wonderful experience for children. They can be encouraged to help build the fire, and once alight, toast marshmallows to have with hot chocolate. Take photographs as you go along to make into a simple book of your trip.

Idea 42

Superhero Experiments

What you need:
Paper with a smooth surface.
White or pale colour wax crayons
Well mixed dark paint

What you do:
Tell the children that you are going to write 'secret messages' today, and show some examples
Write a short 'secret message' clearly on the paper with the crayon. Then paint with a dark colour over the whole page, and your 'secret message' should show clearly through the paint. Allow to dry. You might start by writing children's names, or names of characters.

or

Cover the whole paper with a mixture of crayon scribbles, and/or blocks of colour. Using thick dark paint, paint over the whole page and allow to dry. Using a stick, coin or plastic clay tools, scratch out a design or picture – the paint should come off, leaving the bright crayon marks to show through underneath.

Children can create their own unique superhero character this way

Further Possibilities:
Make some links to some of the reasons why secret codes have been used, and think about other ways of communicating, i.e. Morse code, sign language. Do the children have any special codes with each other? (Some children, boys in particular like to use code words during their imaginative play scenarios)

Use invisible writing to introduce a new idea or story during a group time.

Take the secret message writing a stage further, with some simple experiments – use lemon juice to write a message with a paint brush – when it dries it will become invisible. To reveal the message either place in a warm oven (approx 175 degrees) and check every few minutes till it appears, or warm over a 100 watt light bulb - (obviously take care with heat sources). With some 'superhero powers', clean some dirty copper coins in a small clear dish – soak them in distilled vinegar and a teaspoon of salt, and within moments, they will be looking like shiny new pennies!

Other ideas can be found here: www.yummyscience.co.uk

Idea 43

Wrist bands and Super Belts

What you need:
Kitchen roll tubes, jam jar lids, giant curtain rings (metal or wood), lengths of thick fabric, stickers, glue, clock face with hands.

What you do:

Wrist Bands
Measure the length of the kitchen roll tube with the children. How wide do they want their wrist band to be? Cut the kitchen roll tubes to suit and invite the children to decorate them with pens and stickers. Place a large numerical watch face on the table so that you have something to refer to if the children wish to make watches – these may link to the hero Ben 10. Real watches will provide inspiration and will be of interest. Using a permanent marker help the children mark out numbers on the inside of the jam jar lids. They could add stickers, buttons, etc. Stick the lid (open side up) onto the centre of the piece of tube – you may need to split the tubes so that they fit round wrists, though most children will be able to squeeze their hand through. Wrist bands may act as walkie talkies, or help children change into someone more powerful!

Super Belts
With the children's help, measure and cut the lengths of fabric to fit around their waists (plus a little extra for fastening). Stick, staple or quickly sew one end of fabric around a curtain ring. Invite the children to decorate the fabric belt, which can then be tied around and fastened through the curtain ring. (Thread end through and back on itself)

Discuss with the children whether their belts have any special features? What might these be, and do they need to add anything to the belt to show this?

Further Possibilities:
Ask the children to announce 'Tidy-Up Time in Five Minutes', using their Wrist Bands!
Can they tie their Super Belts to toys to help put them away?
Invite some parents to show the children their watches, perhaps take a quick photograph, and add to a collection of pictures of different watches.
Refer to non-fiction books, i.e. for divers watches, stop watches etc.

Super Cookies

What you need:
A basic biscuit recipe (see below),
Rolling pin, mixing bowl, cookie and gingerbread figure cutters, cake decorations, icing sugar,
Access to a cooker.

Basic Gingerbread Recipe (suitable for vegetarians)
Cooking time about 10 minutes at 170C, Gas mark 3
Makes: 25 Super Figures, or any shapes the children like.

Ingredients

125g unsalted butter.	100g dark muscovado sugar
4 tbsp golden syrup.	325g plain flour
1 tsp bicarbonate of soda	

2 tsp ground ginger, or substitute with cinnamon, or lemon/orange zest
Supercook Writing Icing (optional)

What you do:
Preheat the oven to 170°C, gas mark 3
With children's help when appropriate and safe:
Line baking trays with baking parchment. Melt the butter, sugar and syrup in a medium saucepan, stirring occasionally, and remove from the heat. Sieve flour, bicarbonate of soda and ginger into a bowl and stir the melted ingredients into the dry ingredients to make a stiff dough. Turn out onto a lightly floured surface and roll to a thickness of about 5mm.
Dip biscuit cutters into flour before cutting, and place shapes onto the lined baking trays and bake, in batches, for 9-10 minutes until light golden brown. Remove from the oven. When completely cool, decorate with the icing and cake decorations.
The gingerbread biscuits can be stored in an airtight container for up to two weeks.

Further Possibilities:
Attach rice paper to the cookie figures for capes.
While the biscuits are still warm from the oven, use a chopstick to make a hole in the top and thread on a ribbon for presents or decorations.
Vary the flavours, and ask the children to think about what's different, and how might this have happened? What else could they add? Encourage the children to taste the raw ingredients, and discuss what they like or don't, and how different the biscuits taste when cooked.

Idea 45

Super Play Dough

What you need:

Home-made play dough (see recipe below), blue and black food colouring, fine glitter (not sequins) **No glitter for babies**

Playdough Recipe – cooked

3 cups plain flour
3 cups water
1 1/2 cups salt
3 tablespoons cooking oil
1 tablespoon cream of tartar

You can divide the mix into two (before adding the water and food colouring), or make two batches.

What you do:

Involve the children in measuring, mixing and kneading the play dough – this is particularly pleasurable when the play-dough is still warm. It offers excellent opportunities for directing behaviour in positive ways - for example: children can squeeze, poke, pinch, mash, punch and pull the play dough as much as they like!

To cook, mix all the ingredients together in a large pan, cook over medium heat until mixture pulls away from sides and thickens to play dough consistency.

If you don't have a cooker, don't worry, just add boiling water (include the food colouring here) and mix well with all the dry ingredients. Add glitter and knead well. You'll then have some lovely warm, sparkly superhero play dough. Keeps for 1-2 months in a plastic container.

You might offer a selection of tools, small wooden butter knives, a mincing machine, rolling pins, and perhaps drinking straws cut into pieces. Invite the children to make suggestions about what they would like to use with the play dough. There is no emphasis on a finished product, just experiencing the material.

Further Possibilities

Add oil scents for extra fun (lavender, or food essences - strawberry, orange or lemon)

Save small chocolate boxes and wrappers, and make play dough 'sweeties' with sequins or beads on top

Instead of food colouring, mix 2 tablespoons cheap drinking chocolate with the water, and you'll have wonderful smelling 'chocolate' play dough.

Idea 46

Junk Models
Inspired by ICT

What you need:
A wide selection of heuristic play materials – boxes, cylinders, straws, tubes, cotton reels, corks, string, shells, buttons, beads, scrap pieces of technology, wool cones, fir cones, lolly sticks, small piece of wood, sticks.
Glue, scissors, masking tape, strips of crepe paper etc.
Access to a computer, digital camera, programs specifically designed for young children (See refs below)

What you do:
Plan for an open-ended, well organised junk modelling area. Store some resources in labelled boxes (with a picture too), to encourage the children to become familiar with mathematical language, i.e. cubes, cylinders etc. If possible have space to store models, so children can return and work on them again. A shelf high on the wall will do, to keep the models safe.

Further Possibilities:
To extend the play, you might make some links with ICT – there are many different ideas, here are just a few:
Allow children to use a digital camera to record their model making at different stages. Save the photograph onto the computer and add appropriate labels with a 'text box' feature. Keep the language simple, and use words the children come up with themselves. Print off and display with the model.
Explore different texts and experiment with symbols - 'webdings'. These are installed on the 'fonts' menu and have some great pictures which can be blown up large and printed off.
Investigate story-telling programs - For example, Choose and Tell is good and based on nursery rhymes (see ref below) and enables you to play with rhymes. For example, take Baa Baa Black Sheep off to the beach on a space rocket, or send Humpty Dumpty to a castle in a boat!

An excellent website specifically for early years children, lots of ideas and good information: http://foundation.e2bn.org/
Choose and Tell – Nursery Rhymes – playing with rhymes www.inclusive.co.uk.

Idea 47

Table Top Prints

What you need:

Powder paint in different colours – these will link to children's interests and favourite characters.

Sheets of paper - white, black, bright yellow, orange and greens work well.

A table top, aprons, and a bowl of warm soapy water nearby, with an old towel.

What you do:

Together with the children, sprinkle the powder paint onto the surface of a clean table. Add small amounts of water using your fingers, little sponges or a plant spray. Engage with the children through open-ended questions, e.g. 'What happens if we mix the water with the powder? What do you think is happening to the colours? What might happen if we add a different colour/more water? etc. Experiment together – what patterns and shapes occur? Whilst some colours are still separate on the table, carefully lay a sheet of paper on top and peel it off slowly – it is always interesting to compare the print with the surface of the table. You might invite the children to draw favourite characters or superheroes in the paint, or depict a story that they have been playing.

Further Possibilities:

Use balloons to pick up the paint from the table, and then print from the balloons onto paper nearby.

Have squares of fabric made from old sheets, and print on these – you can add collage later and display the artwork, or make into capes.

If children are interested in developing letters, try writing these in the paint, or scribe words that the children request.

Add corn flour to the paint mixture and see what happens!

Idea 48

Map Making

What you need:

Large sheets of paper

Coloured wool

Digital camera

Pencils and pens, coloured sticky paper

Glue and sticky labels

What you do:

The children may already be interested and curious about maps. You might introduce a new addition, perhaps by using 'Super Beat Baby' or a puppet the children know and love. The puppet or Super Beat Baby cannot find their way across the outdoor space/from the nursery/from the newsagents shop to the garden gate etc. They need help. Could the children draw some maps to show them the way? Children may wish to dress the part, as Super-Map Makers! Begin by making a real journey and take photographs of important landmarks along the way. This works well if you can print the photographs off fairly swiftly, to keep the interest alive. You can look at the pictures together and order them in the right sequence. You might use the photographs to illustrate your map, or encourage the children to draw the route and illustrate it. The maps can be rolled up and tied with bright ribbons.

Further Possibilities:

Consider introducing a programmable robot which you could use to travel around the map or the outdoor area. For example:
A Bee-Bot is a programmable floor robot that has been purpose-built for use with Early Phase and Primary students. Their features include:

- Sounds and flashing eyes that let students know that their instructions have been entered;
- The ability to remember up to 40 instructions / steps entered by children;
- The ability to move accurately in 15cm steps and to turn in 90° increments;
- Bright buttons for the children to use to input instructions;
- A friendly and happy design that appeals to young learners (and teachers!).

Further information can be found at: http://www.tts-group.co.uk/Bee-Bot
https://www.learningplace.com.au/deliver/content.asp?pid=38840

You might send a letter from Captain Blue Beard, the fearsome Pirate, who describes a spot on the maps where treasure is buried. Get the children to draw an X that marks the spot on the map and a picture of the treasure. Meanwhile, hide plastic or real coins for the children to find.

Idea 49

Peek-a-boo Book

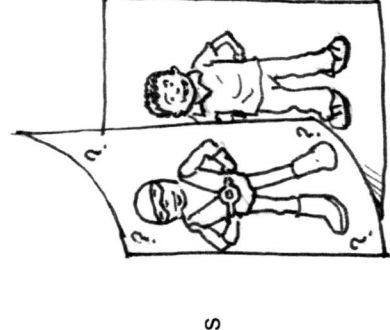

What you need:

Paper, card, pens, sellotape or glue.
Dressing up clothes. Belts, jewellery, fabric lengths, hats, wigs etc
Photographs of the children dressed up, and photographs of them in ordinary clothes.
The photographs can be printed cheaply on paper. The dressing up does not need to be in 'bought' costumes though, by all means use these if you have them and the children wish to. Do offer, a rich variety of open-ended dressing-up materials in order that the children can design and make their own outfits, or add accessories to the shop-bought ones.
You might also provide face paints and time to make simple masks.

What you do:

The idea is to make a simple 'lift-the-flap' book rather like the 'Where's Spot' books but, instead of Spot, the children are hiding. Have a photograph of each child dressed in ordinary clothes *under* the flaps, and a photograph of them in their dressing-up costume *on top of* the flap.
You can choose a title for the book together, - e.g. 'Can you guess who I am?' or 'Where are the children?' This concept supports the children in acknowledging the differences between real and imaginary.
Depending on how many children there are, you might have one flap per page, or two or three. Children can choose their card for the flap, stick in their photographs, and do some mark making on the page. It does not need to be neat and tidy!
Always leave a few spare pages to add new photographs. You can bind the book by hole-punching the left hand or top margin and tying with a strong ribbon, or staple it. If you staple the book cover the staples with strong tape, as they lift and can get sharp over time. When you glue the dressed-up figure onto the flap, leave space for the flap to be stuck down, and to bend as you lift it.

Further Possibilities:

Make sure the book is available for the children to read by themselves. Encourage them to show off their book, particularly if you are in a setting with more than one group/class, e.g. arrange for them to go and show the book to other groups or classes. Likewise, encourage them to show it to parents and family. Develop computer keyboard skills – touching keys gently but firmly, not holding them down, in order to type a title for the book. Add who the authors are, putting each child's name on the front, i.e. 'Written by *names of children…*' is great. You might add photographs of practitioners or the setting's pets or puppets.
Every so often children may like to update their costume, so just add a new picture.
An alternative to the book is to create an interactive display. On a notice board or wall space, stick your photographs and flaps, with the appropriate text and a title. The display would need to be at the right height for children to reach easily.

Idea 50

The Superheroes Hospital

What you need:
A space to set up a simple role-play area – if possible a covered outdoor space. Even the side of an indoor corridor will do!

Resources might include:
Home made bandages and slings (from old sheets/pillow cases) and a few real crepe bandages, etc.

Small mattresses, blankets and pillows for beds. Green fabric to hang as a screen/curtain. Clip boards, paper and squared paper, a small white board or black board with pens/chalk. Card to make into signs. Lengths of wood for crutches, or even some real crutches?

Plastic cups, jug, plates, food, kettle, trays

Dustpan and brush, small plastic bottles (for medicine).

Wheelie buggy or trolley to use as an ambulance

Small white aprons, caps, green and white shirts.

First aid kit, stethoscopes, pretend injections – you can usually get real syringes from a health centre, though obviously without the needle!

What you do:
If superheroes are about, there will undoubtedly be the odd bump, scrape and collision. It can be one of the difficulties for practitioners in allowing this play. The superhero hospital is an appropriate and contextual way to respond, and will support children to take care of each other, building awareness between real hurts and pretend ones. The resources listed are intended to spark your own ideas. It will be the interactions and interventions between practitioners and children that form the crucial part of the play.

Indeed, you may include yourself as one of the first patients! Practice tying slings and bandages with the children.

Make signs with the children to hang up in the hospital, and model writing 'patient notes' with the clipboards and squared paper.

Further Possibilities:
Provide solid torches, with green or blue transparency paper over the end to make your flashing siren lights.

Find a recording of siren noises

Add books & stories about hospitals, rescues etc.

Invite parents/visitors involved in health care into your setting. Plan a visit to local GP surgery.

SAMPLE OF A SUPERHERO / WEAPON PLAY POLICY

Name of Setting

Superhero and Weapon Play Policy

Policy Statement

We recognise that each child is unique and will support them to be resilient, capable, confident and self assured. Children learn to be strong and independent from a base of secure and loving relationships, as well as having the opportunity to learn in a positive and stimulating environment. (*Or a similar introduction linked to your curriculum document*)

At (*name of setting*) we aim to provide support for all areas of learning. From time to time, children may show an interest in superhero and weapon play.

Rationale

Historically, this type of play has often been banned from early year's settings, in the belief that it encourages aggression or violence. This ban, as well as being difficult to enforce, may well have a negative impact on young children's development, particularly boys.

Recent research and current writing suggests that children learn important lessons by exploring these themes in the safe arena of play. For example, concepts such as good and evil, life and death, strength and power, gender and identity. Children have the means through this sort of play to express themselves, their lives, and their individual experiences.

We have developed this policy in order to support practitioners and parents to respond appropriately to superhero and weapon play. If there are concerns about aggressive or threatening behaviour, we will refer to our Behaviour Management Policy.

SAMPLE OF THE AIMS AND OBJECTIVES

Name of Setting

Superhero and Weapon Play Policy

Aims and Objectives

- No toy weapons will be allowed in the setting. Children will be asked to store these toys on their pegs, or in the 'going home box'.

- We will encourage children to be creative with their ideas. If they wish to *make* weapons, a selection of open-ended materials, i.e. wood work or construction/junk modelling, are available for this purpose.

- Children may wear 'superhero' costumes. We will provide a rich variety of dress-up materials and accessories, in order that children may develop their play further.

- Children will be supported to play co-operatively, and develop an awareness of the needs and feelings of others.

- Children, who do not wish to play, will be supported to say No, and find appropriate language, i.e. "If I'm not in your game, don't shoot me".

- Clear limits will be set to keep play safe. If someone gets hurt, (emotionally or physically) we will help the children to resolve their differences, and find ways to make amends.

- In order to support children's developing skills – communication, language, personal, social and emotional, we will involve them in creating 'safe rules' for play. This will include brainstorming, discussion and practitioners joining the play occasionally.

- We welcome parents' views, comments and observations. Please do not hesitate to discuss any queries or concerns with us.

List of useful Books and Resources

Further Reading - Books mentioned in text

Biddulph, S (2003) Raising Boys Thorsons ISBN-10: 0007153694 & ISBN-13: 978-0007153695

Bromley, H (2002) 50 Exciting Ways to Use a Builder's Tray - Lawrence Educational – ISBN 978-1-903670-15-6

Garrick, R (2006) Minibeasts and more' - Young children investigating the natural world - Early Education

Holland, P (2003) We Don't Play with Guns Here: War, Weapon and Superhero Play in the Early Years - Open University Press ISBN-10: 0335210899 & ISBN-13: 978-0335210893

Hoffman, E (2004) Magic Capes, Amazing Powers Transforming Superhero Play in the Classroom - Redleaf Press

Hyder, T (2005) 'War, Conflict and Play' (2005), Open University Press Debating Play Series edited by Tina Bruce ISBN-10: 0335212999 & ISBN-13: 978-0335212996

Levin, D.E & Carlsson-Paige, N. (2004) 2nd Edition The War Play Dilemma - Teachers College Press

Paley G V (1986) Boys and Girls: Superheros in the Doll Corner - The University of Chicago Press

Articles

'Engaging Boys in the Early Years' by Tracy Smith, Early Years Foundation Stage Team Islington http://www.islington.gov.uk/DownloadableDocuments/EducationandLearning/Pdf/PSEYT_engaging_boys_early

'Confident, capable and creative: supporting boys' achievements' www.standards.dcsf.gov.uk Primary National Strategy http://publications.teachernet.gov.uk/eOrderingDownload/DCSF-00682-2007.pdf

Beyond Banning War and Superhero Play - Meeting Children's Needs in Violent Times ,Diane E. Levin (2003) http://www.lesley.edu/academic_centers/peace/content/warandsuperhero.pdf

'Understanding Aggressive Toys' article via National Toy Council http://www.btha.co.uk/pdfs/aggressive_toys.pdf

Resources & Web Sites

ICT – Excellent Web site with information and Ideas for early years - http://foundation.e2bn.org/

Popular Culture CBBC website list of all character http://www.bbc.co.uk/cbeebies/characters/

Lyrics to all CBBC songs:-
http://search.bbc.co.uk/search?q=words&x=24&y=14&scope=cbeebies&tab=CBEEBIES&recipe=cbeebies

Choose and Tell – Nursery Rhymes www.inclusive.co.uk Inclusive technology Tel: 01457 819790

Programmable robot – 'Bee-Bot' http://www.tts-group.co.uk/Bee-Bot

Local Libraries for unusual tapes & CDs i.e. weather sounds, birdsong and world music, Disney themes/popular culture

Beat babies – Lawrence Educational - www.educationalpublications.com

Resources & Web Sites

Excellent selection world Music from www.putumayokids.com

Drumming Music –Japanese Kodo Drummers , STOMP, Salif Keita or Miriam Makeba

Haberdashers for colourful dancing ribbons, and cheap, but colourful lining fabric for capes and movement work.

£1 shops for cheap gift bags to make themed resources, literacy materials

Blank 'explosion' signs can be found on the Times Educational Supplement website, register for free to access teacher resources, articles, forums – http://www.tes.co.uk/article.aspx?storycode=6001151

Web address to see a comprehensive list of superhero story-books http://www.amazon.com/Super-Hero-Stories/lm/RHM1OAC6HEYAP

Birds RSPB 'Royal Society for the Protection of Birds' http://shopping.rspb.org.uk/c/SingingBirds.htm

The Helicopter Technique – information based on work of Vivian Gussin Paley www.makebelievearts.co.uk

Children's Story Books   *Listed under emotions/themes*

Loneliness
Aldo by John Burningham
Leon and Bob by Simon James

Heroes
The Paper bag Princess by Robert N. Munsch
Isabel's Noisy Tummy David McKee
Cannonball Simp and Borka, the goose with no feathers both by John Burningham
Frog is a Hero by Max Velthuijs
The Turtle and the Island – A folk tale from Papua New Guinea retold by Barbara Ker Wilson
Amazing Grace by Mary Hoffman

Prejudice
Frog in Love and Frog and the Stranger Max Velthuijs
An Angel just Like Me by Mary Hoffman

Fear (and Excitement)
Frog is Frightened! Max Velthuijs
Shhh! By Sally Grindley and Peter Utton
A Dark Dark Tale by Ruth Brown
Bimwili and the Zimwi by Verna Aardema

Children's Story Books *Listed under emotions/themes*

Superheroes & Boys
Billy's Bucket by Kes Gray & Garry Parsons
Hue Boy by Caroline Binch
Max by Bob Graham
Traction Man is Here by Mini Grey

Anger & Bullying
Angry Arthur by Hiawyn Oram
Bootsie Barker Bites by Barbara Bottner, Peggy Rathmann
Tyrone the Horrible & Tyrone and the Swamp Gang by Hans Wilhelm

Adventure
OY! Get off our Train! by John Burningham
The Three Little Wolves and the Big Bad Pig by Eugene Trivizas
We're going on a Bear Hunt by Helen Oxenbury
The Very Busy Spider by Eric Carle
Wendel's Workshop by Chris Riddell (Macmillan Children's Books 2007)
The Lighthouse Keeper's Lunch by Ronda and David Armitage
Harry and the Bucketful of Dinosaurs by Ian Whybrow and Adrian Reynolds
Mr Gumpy's Outing by John Burningham
Do Pirates take Baths? By Kathy Tucker Albert Whitman & Company 1997
Man on the Moon (a day in life of Bob) by Simon Bartram Templar Publishing 2002

We hope you have found this publication useful.   Other titles in our 'Exciting Things To Do' series are:

BUILDER'S TRAY	50 ways to use a Builder's Tray	978-1-903670-15-6
LET'S EXPLORE	50 starting points for science activities	978-1-903670-11-8
LET'S BUILD	50 exciting ideas for construction play	978-1-903670-30-9
LET'S MOVE & DANCE	50 exciting starting points for Music & Dance	978-1-903670-35-4
LET'S WRITE	50 starting points for writing experiences	978-1-903670-10-1
LITERACY OUTDOORS	50 starting points for outdoor literacy experiences	978-1-903670-53-8
MATHS OUTDOORS	50 exciting ways to develop mathematical awareness	978-1-903670-61-3
MATHS THROUGH STORIES	50 exciting ideas for developing maths through stories	978-1-903670-46-0
NURSERY RHYMES	50 nursery rhymes to play with	978-1-903670-23-1
OUTSIDE	50 exciting things to do outside	978-1-903670-07-1
PICTURE THIS	50 ways to use a camera in early years settings	978-1-903670-22-4
PLANT AN IDEA	50 exciting ways to use flowers, trees and plant life	978-1-903670-24-8
SCIENCE OUTDOORS	50 exciting ideas for outdoor science activities	978-1-903670-67-5
SMALL WORLD RECIPE BOOK	50 exciting ideas for small world play	978-1-903670-39-2
STORYBOXES	50 exciting ideas for storyboxes	978-1-903670-16-3
STORYLINES	50 ideas for using large puppets, dolls & soft toys	978-1-903670-06-4
SUPERHEROES & POPULAR CULTURE	50 exciting ideas for using superheroes & popular culture	978-1-903670-79-8

For details on these and all our other early years resources visit our website: www.LawrenceEducational.com